The Hidden Jewel

Javon A. Frazier

ISBN-13: 978-1500135430

All scripture references are noted from the New International Version of The Holy Bible unless otherwise noted

DEDICATION

This book is dedicated to my two little men, Malik and Cambrin. I thank God for deeming me worthy enough to be your mother. You two are my world, my blessings, my everything. I love you and I want you to know that you can achieve anything you want, as long as you allow God to lead you.

CONTENTS

ACKNOWLEDGMENTS

First and foremost, I want to start by thanking my Heavenly Father. Without Him, I would not be here and this book would not be possible. Even when I wanted to curse God and die, His grace and mercy would not let me go. God gets all the glory!

There are so many people that I want to thank, so many people who have loved and supported me unconditionally. To my three guardian angels: Tyeasha, Grandma Granger and Ma Carol- I love you and miss you more than words could ever express. Although God saw fit to take you from this earth, I still remember everything you three have ever done or said to help break down my walls. Your living was not in vain. To my angel on earth, Aunt Tonya- thank you for never giving up on me. You have saved my life so many times and I am eternally grateful that God loved me enough to bring you into my life. To my father- thank you for always supporting me and making me believe that I can do anything. You are my superman. To my grandmothers, Diane and Phyllis- thank you for showing me what real women of God look like. I love you both. To my mom and my sisters- You guys are my foundation. I cherish every memory that we have created and I look forward to creating many more. I love you to the moon and back.

A special thank you to my sister/mentor/friend, Tiffany Bethea- the words "thank you" are not adequate enough to express my gratitude. Thank you for taking a chance on me without knowing anything about me. Thank you for being there, for believing in me, and for pushing me forward even though I wanted to stay in the background. I love you always. To Ms. Kimmoly- what can I say? Thank you for being my brain. With your help, my thoughts are now a reality. You are awesome! Last, but certainly not least my beautiful pastor, Dr. Karen Bethea- I cannot express how much I love and appreciate you. God knew exactly what He was doing when He sent me to STCFOC!

-Javon

1

INTRODUCTION

I'm writing this book for several reasons. The first reason is to help others. I've been through so much in my life and I finally realize that it was all for a purpose. The next reason is to free myself. Although I know that everything happened for a reason, I still hurt in some areas. This is a healing process for me. There will be some moments that will make us cry, there will be moments that will make us remember things that we tried to forget. But in the end, WE will be healed. For so long, it has been laid on my heart to write this book, but I was afraid. Afraid that people would look at me differently. Afraid that my family, one person in particular, would resent me. To be honest, I'm still afraid, even as I write this. But I am up for the challenge, especially if it means helping someone else. Thank you for taking this journey with me.

2
MY CHILDHOOD

So, where do I begin? I guess the best place would be the beginning. I was born in Georgetown, South Carolina to two high school sweethearts, depending on who you ask. According to my mother, he wasn't ready or excited and neither was his family, but they were in love. According to my father, my mother was a "jump-off" or easy. He wasn't sure that he was the father and he wasn't about to raise another man's baby. I still don't really know the truth, but it doesn't matter. I love both of my parents more than anyone will ever know, despite what happened.

The beginning of my childhood was a normal, wonderful one. I don't remember much of my life before my mother went to college. I have memories of always being with her, no matter where she went, but I imagine that was after she graduated, considering she had me at 15. While my mom was in college, I lived with my dad's parents in a small country house

2

surrounded by pigs, plum trees and family and filled with love. Every Sunday morning, we would gather in the front room for family prayer. My aunt and uncle also lived with us. My uncle was my favorite person on that side of the family. I remember following him and his friends around everywhere. We would catch tadpoles and dragonflies. I was quite the little tomboy, although you wouldn't know it now. Even then, I knew I was different. I had a cousin that was the doll of the family. She had the best clothes and the prettiest hair bows and everyone loved her. The teachers always complimented her and gave her special treatment. Even at a young age, I felt out of place, like I wasn't good enough. I don't know if it had something to do with my mom, but outside of my grandma's house, my dad's family wasn't very friendly.

My mom came home on the weekends and sometimes I went back to her campus with her. I remember being the doll baby on campus. My dad was...... you know, I really don't know where he was. Don't get me wrong, he came around. But it was more like he was a visiting relative, not my father. I later realized that this had a major impact on my life- not just relationships. I remember being at a service recently where the speaker said "If your father wasn't there, it effects your relationship with God." That's when it clicked, but we'll get back to that later.

Back to my mother, because as you will see as we move along, my mother is an important piece of the puzzle that is *"me"*. My mom was amazing. She was so fun and beautiful and strong; she was my hero, my best friend. I remember seeing her fight someone (her cousin actually) and thinking that my mother was the best mommy in the world. Now that may sound funny, but I knew that my mommy would always protect me. That all I had to do was say "I'm gonna tell my momma" and everything would be ok. Boy was I wrong.

While my mother was in college, she had another baby girl. The details are a little fuzzy surrounding my sister's birth, but I remember being happy to have a little sister. I'm not sure when we all came back and lived together as a family, because I know there was a time that she lived with her grandmother and I lived with mine. But I know we lived together when she was a toddler, because I remember her climbing out of her crib all the time.

When I was about 7, I can't remember the time frame exactly, my mom moved to Wilmington, North Carolina and eventually we moved with her. We moved in with my great uncle, which was a good thing. He was an elder in the church and a good role model. He was the father figure that we never had. Whenever I had a nightmare, I would go into his room and cry. He would pray with me (he always prayed) and hug me until I calmed down.

Two things about both sides of my family: they are very religious and musically talented. My family is full of singers, pastors, ministers, musicians, producers, etc. So naturally, music and church are in my blood. We went to a great church and I loved the music there. I was a member of the choir, which was under the direction of the Pastor's son. We'll call him "Darrius".

"Darrius" was awesome. He was a great father, he made his own music and he loved me. Oh I wanted to be in his family so bad! And I was. Wherever he went, I was there. People were calling me his daughter and I loved it. I felt like I was a part of something. I performed with him at local churches all around town, and was even featured on his records. He had a dance group and I was the youngest. I was always in front, singing and dancing my little heart out! My mom let me go with him whenever I wanted. His wife loved me too, so it was a match. I spent more time with him and his family than I did at home. His children became my little brothers and sisters. Being with him was everything to me. I had a complete family and I was able to fulfill my passion for music.

Eventually things with "Darrius" began to change. It started out with his "special hugs" as he called it. He would hug me and touch me in inappropriate places or sit me on his lap and grind me against his pelvis. I knew something was wrong, but I didn't say anything because that was my daddy, so to speak. He even did it in church. I remember one day, we were at the church for rehearsal or something. Everyone had left and we were the only ones. "Darrius" pulled me to the side and said he wanted to give me his special hug. There we were, on the floor of the back row in the sanctuary. "Darrius" was on top of me, grinding and kissing me. I think at this point, I was about nine. He never touched me under my clothes, but it was just as bad. This would go on for years. I never questioned it. I mean, naturally I didn't like it. But the love and attention that he showed me was so wonderful, it overshadowed the other things. I mean, it wasn't like he was harming me, right?

By this time, my mom was dating the man that would later become her husband. We'll call him "Xavier". "Xavier" was a young guy, I think like 17 or something. He seemed to be a good person. He always played with us and took us places, so I didn't spend as much time with "Darrius" anymore. "Xavier" moved in with us and they got married. We were a family! Momma was so happy, we all were. Things were great.

Eventually, my uncle moved out and left us the house and that's when things really took a turn for the worse. Momma and "Xavier" starting fighting a lot. He was cheating, stealing her jewelry, etc. I don't remember when he started touching me exactly, but I think it was after my mom had another baby. It was like it started all of a sudden. So not only did I have to deal with "Darrius", but now "Xavier". I swear it was like they were in competition with each other. But the thing that made it so difficult was the fact that they were both still so loving and fun at times. So naturally, I was confused. I thought that was how people showed love. And I couldn't tell anyone because I didn't want momma to be mad at me. Even though they always fought, it was clear that she loved "Xavier". And I didn't want to tell on "Darrius", because I loved him. His family loved me. And he was the Pastor's son. So I dealt with it. All at the age of ten. Imagine that.

"Xavier" started getting more aggressive. He started making comments and feeling on me more. He even made me feel on him. His was the first penis that I ever encountered in my life. I remember it like it was yesterday. We were riding in the car and he started talking about sex. I think at this time I was in the fourth or fifth grade. Now mind you, this is the same guy that wouldn't let me take sex education in school. He didn't let me go to school dances or talk to boys and he was always monitoring what I wore. Very over-protective. Now that I'm older, I feel like he was trying to keep me to himself. But back to the conversation in the car. He asked me what I knew about sex and if I had ever seen a penis. Of course I said no. He asked if I wanted to see one, of course I said no. I wasn't interested in boys like that. That was the end of that until we got home. At this time, we lived in a two story townhouse. The couch was adjacent to the stairs. I was sitting on the couch and he called my name. I looked up and there was my "daddy", standing there with his penis out! I screamed and covered my eyes. He went back upstairs, and called me to him. He was in the bathroom doorway with the lights off. He told me to give him my hand and then he did it. He made me touch his penis. I was so disgusted. I couldn't say anything because I really didn't know how to respond. I felt so dirty, so guilty, so confused. Later, he told me that he did it because he wanted me to be ready for the world, but that it had to be our little secret because no one would understand.

3
THE CHANGE

After that, I changed. I became quiet, and very moody. I had so much going on in my head. My life was hell. I couldn't tell anyone what I was going through. They started saying I had a bad attitude. And I did. I could be smiling one minute and then frowning the next, but there was a reason. No one noticed the little gestures that he made, the way he looked at me. He was always finding a reason to punish me; that was his time to get his feel in. Of course my mother was the type to "let the man be the man" so he was in charge. I was in hell. I wanted to die! At this time, my father married someone and started coming around more, but he still wasn't there as much as I needed him to be. "Xavier" was there when I cried over my father, he even dried my tears. He took us downtown for ice cream and pizza, which was our favorite thing to do with him. I was so tortured. How could someone be such a great daddy one minute and such a monster the next? Then of course there was still "Darrius", doing the same thing. Can you imagine what that was like? I wanted to be loved, wanted a daddy. But I was stuck with a part time father, a step dad that was a monster and "Darrius".

One day, momma asked me what was wrong. She asked if "Darrius" had ever touched me. I cried and told her yes. To this day, I don't know why I didn't tell her about "Xavier" too. That was my moment to end it all. I would tell my momma and she would protect me. Make it all better. But I still couldn't tell her about "Xavier". I guess it was my fear. Or maybe it was my love for her and the need to keep my family together that stopped me. I don't know. Momma called "Xavier" and told him what I had said about "Darrius". Can you believe he was angry? Ha! According to momma, he punched the glass of the phone booth he was using. Now that I'm older, I wonder about that. Was he really mad that someone had hurt me, or was it because someone else was touching what belonged to him? I guess I'll never know.

After I told my mom, things changed. A lot. It became common knowledge at the church. I think my mom had a meeting with the pastor but I don't know what was said. I later heard that "Darrius" told other members of the youth group that my stepdad was trying to pin the blame on him to take focus off of what he was doing. Laughable. So "Xavier" was mad at "Darrius" and "Darrius" was mad at "Xavier". And both were guilty of the same crime...

School was the only place that I felt free. Ok, let me rephrase that. *The classroom was the only place that I felt free.* I loved reading and writing. That was my escape. I would read books that were way above my level. I even read my mother's books. She had a huge collection of Harlequin Romance novels. Maybe that's why we (meaning my mother and I) had such a twisted view on love. We were stuck in a fantasy world.

Outside of the classroom was a different story. I never fit in, no matter how hard I tried. I didn't dress the way that the other girls did because my mom couldn't afford it. I didn't move like they moved or talk like they talked. The only thing that we had in common was music. We would sing on the playground during lunch and recess, they loved to hear me sing. There was one girl that I really liked. We'll call her Rochelle. Rochelle was one of the popular kids. She was perfect. Pretty, long hair, nice clothes, and all the boys liked her. Our relationship was a weird one. We considered ourselves best friends. I stayed at her house, she stayed at mine. I called her mother "Mommy" and vice versa. But when we got to school, she ignored me like the rest of the girls. Everywhere I went, it seemed like I was the outcast. Home, school, church, etc. I quickly learned that the best way to act like it didn't bother me was to always have an attitude. Keep people out. It was my defense mechanism and it is one that I'm still trying to break.

We switched churches, sometime between elementary and middle school. One of my mom's friends from the old church was starting a new one and we were his first members. It was a small family church, but I loved it. My mother taught Sunday school and ran the choir. I was always singing lead, me and the Pastor's son. When I was about 10, I gave my first sermon and became a Junior Missionary. Both of my parents became ministers too.

Other than living with my grandmother, this was the happiest time of my childhood. Although things were not perfect at home, they were a lot better. I was so sold out for Jesus that nothing mattered. I had so much faith in God that it didn't matter what we went through as a family, I knew it would be ok. My step-dad wasn't messing with me anymore and "Darrius" was no longer in my life. I finally felt like I fit in. It was like once I accepted God and my calling, everything was so much better. My family was very supportive and proud of me. Why wouldn't they be? I was following in the footsteps of the "family way." At home, we had family bible study and my love for God was increasing. He was speaking to me and I knew His voice. I remember one night in particular, I was upstairs working on a sermon. I went downstairs to share my message with my mother (I always went to her for advice about my walk with God). When I got downstairs, I found my parents at the table, my mother had her head in her hands. When I shared what God had given me, tears filled her eyes. She said that she needed to hear that. My message spoke to her directly. It was at that moment that I knew God was real and I was called to do his work.

4
FIRE

To be honest, I don't remember when my step dad began messing with me again, but I know it was after my baby sister was born. It was a gradual change. It started with him just watching me. I would wake up to him standing at my door. Then he advanced to touching me. He would act like he was putting covers over me and would "sneak a feel." It became so routine that I was afraid to sleep by myself, I had my little sisters sleep with me. My bed was small, so there was no room for him to feel on me when they were in the bed. Well he fixed that. He made a rule that we all had to sleep in our own beds. Ha! Talk about abusing power. Nothing was safe anymore. It was as if he didn't care about what he did or that I saw him. He would even look in my window while I dressed. It got to the point that my little sister had to be my bodyguard. She would keep him occupied while I took a shower and got dressed. It was horrible.

There are so many stories that I could tell about this time. So many traumatic experiences that come to mind when I think about my childhood. Every day was a cycle of molestation and abuse, in one form or another. He was either watching me or touching me. That's all I knew. But on the flip side, it was also filled with wonderful moments. My family didn't have a lot of money, so my parents were always finding new and inexpensive ways to bond and have fun. We would walk downtown or catch the bus to different places. We had movie night on the weekends and "Xavier" was even teaching me how to cook. I felt like I could never tell anyone what was going on. The family would be destroyed and it would be my fault. Even as a child, I had an adult mentality. Even though we had parents, I felt like it was my job to protect everyone. I felt like I had to be strong for my mom and my sisters. I would take the abuse, because at least he wasn't messing with my sisters. I took on so much as a child that I never had a childhood.

This went on for many years, and my mom and "Xavier" fought A LOT. Things were rough. We were always moving because "Xavier" wasn't paying the bills like he was supposed to. He really wasn't much of a man, in my opinion. The only thing you could count on was a good meal- that man knew he could cook!

As I stated before, we moved around a lot. I went to four elementary schools, two middle schools and two high schools. That is horrible. I would imagine all of that relocating has contributed to me being such an introvert. I didn't waste time making friends because we were always leaving. Besides, I couldn't bring friends over anyway. I remember a time when I had my best friend sleep over. Of course she knew about the situation, so we already planned for her to sleep on the outside of the bed. I didn't think he would come in because I had company. Needless to say, I was wrong. How embarrassing! I cried and cried; being the good friend that she was, she hugged me and promised to keep it a secret. I never wanted to have anyone over again.

When I was about 12, my mom left "Xavier" and we moved back to our hometown in South Carolina. It was a happy day for me, being so close to my family. Not to mention the fact that we were free from hell. We had to move back in with my grandmother, but at least we didn't have the arguing and fighting that we had in Wilmington. My mom seemed happier too, she was even dating.

"Xavier" moved to SC shortly after, but he didn't live with us. It wasn't until we got our own place that he moved in with us. At first, everything was normal; like it was in the beginning. Then he started touching and watching me again. I was a little more developed at this time, but not much. Either way, it was enough for him. He didn't try to hide the fact that he was watching me. I remember one night in particular. My mom was out with her girlfriends, and my sisters and I were home with "Xavier". I think they had been arguing, because "Xavier" was in the room getting drunk. I went in the room to ask if we could get some ice cream and he asked me to come in and close the door. He started talking about some nonsense about him and my mom, then he asked if he could touch my bra. I was so shocked, of course I said no. Then he asked if he could touch my panties, as if that was better! I said no and left. That night I had my two sisters sleep with me. The next day, my mom and "Xavier" got into a huge fight and the cops had to be called. When I told my mom what happened, she went crazy! It was in the papers and everything. I remember my cousin blaming me when he read the paper and questioning if I was sure that he really tried something. I couldn't believe it! I thought we were done with "Xavier" finally, but he got out and came right back. My mom called our Pastor to the house to counsel us. Would you believe that they were talking to me as if I made it up! It was like no one believed me. I got so tired of dealing with things by myself that I told my Aunt what was going on. Naturally she wanted to get me out of that situation, but I begged her not to tell anyone especially not my Uncle. I knew that would be trouble. She kept it to herself, but all of a sudden, she needed a baby sitter every summer. So, every summer, I was off to Maryland. Freedom! When she first mentioned it, "Xavier" had a fit! He kept insisting that she take my other sisters. He said "you can't have this one. Not this one..."

Let me just tell you, even when you don't understand what is going on, God is in control. My favorite scripture is Jeremiah 29:11: *"For I know the thoughts that I think toward you, saith the Lord, thoughts of peace and not evil, to give you an expected end."* There is a reason for everything. Nothing happens by chance, you are NOT a mistake. No matter what the circumstances were surrounding your conception, God had a plan for you. There IS an expected end. It took me years to understand this. Which is why I'm finally able to write this book. I understand that everything that happened had a purpose. Some things were God ordained, some were because of Javon. In the end, everything happened for a reason.

Ok, I got off subject for a minute, but I really felt led to say that at that moment. You will see that this book is like nothing that you've ever read before. I am being so transparent, because I want to be healed completely. But more importantly, I want YOU to be healed completely. God wants us to be whole so we can function in the way He designed us. Life happens to us all, but Jesus came to redeem us. To revive us, to restore us. You can be healed, and better than before. Trust me, I know. I don't look like what I've been through.

5
INVISIBLE

Let's fast forward to high school, because the years from age 12 until then consisted of the same thing; hell at home, summers in Maryland. By this time, I had a HORRIBLE attitude and no real friends, but I excelled in school. I was a member of DECA, an Association of Marketing Students. In DECA, we traveled all over the country competing against other students. Throughout my career as a DECA student, I won at the regional, state and national levels. I was definitely not the typical teenager. While others were going to dances and games, I was studying or going to church. Even with all that, I was still misunderstood. I was very mature for my age and not necessarily by choice. When I wasn't taking care of my little sisters, I was worried about things I couldn't control: my mother and "Xavier" fighting, bills not being paid, or watching my back. People would look at my maturity level and accuse me of being "grown" or "fast." I remember one Sunday after church I was talking to my first lady. I forgot what the subject was, but I remember her saying, "I know you're not a virgin." I was shocked, but that wasn't the worst part. When I told her that I was a virgin, she made me swear on the Bible! I couldn't believe it. It was as if my word wasn't enough. That hurt me more than I think she realized. Unfortunately, she was not the only one with this misconception. Once people heard about what happened with "Darrius" and "Xavier", they assumed I was fast and I either lied or I did something to provoke them. Never mind the fact that I was a child in both situations.

It seemed like everywhere I went, I had to defend myself against adults. The women thought I was fast and the men thought I was easy. One time in particular, I was at church for a cookout. There was a store across the street and I was admiring the dress in the window. The deacon of our church saw me admiring the dress and said "you like that dress?" When I said yes, he asked what I was willing to do for that dress. Although I couldn't believe he would say something like that, I wasn't shocked. I looked at him, rolled my eyes and responded "babysit your children."

During this time, my father was on wife number two. She had a daughter that was around the same age, so I spent more time with them in Georgia. My father was the owner of his own construction company, one of the largest minority owned companies in the south. His wife worked for Delta, so between the two, flying was not an issue. Whenever there was a major event at my step sister's school, I was there. Homecoming, Valentine's Dance, etc. That was the part of high school I actually enjoyed. My step father didn't allow me to go to games or dances, so I went to Georgia every chance I got.

There was a down side to spending so much time in Georgia, however: my step sister got all the attention. We spent a lot of time around her family and she was very spoiled by everyone, including my father. I guess it didn't help that she was very pretty with long hair and a popular cheerleader. I never felt good enough when she was around. She didn't do anything to make me feel that way; to be honest, she was an awesome big sister. She gave me my first lessons on makeup and fashion. I remember sitting in the bathroom watching her do her hair and put on makeup. I wanted to be just like her; do what she did, have the attention she had. To this day, I still love her very much and I'm so proud of the woman she has become. Back then, I think I created this idea in my head: *I wasn't good enough. I wasn't popular enough, my daddy loved her more than he loved me.* Even though I loved gong to Georgia, I was guaranteed to end up crying before the end of the trip. No matter what I did, no matter how many A's I earned or how many DECA competitions I won, it was never acknowledged. But let my sister win a cheerleading competition; it would be celebration time. I believe in my heart that my father didn't intentionally ignore me, he just didn't understand me. He was used to having people around him for his money and what he could do for them. He would leave money on my dresser every morning for shopping while he went to work. But I didn't want his money, I wanted his time. I don't think he understood that. I think he loved me the best way he knew how, but because it was not what I needed, I felt like he didn't care. He didn't know what was going on at home, so he didn't know how much I needed my daddy. At home I was abused, ignored, overlooked, overworked, and misunderstood. In Georgia, I was ignored, overlooked, misunderstood and miserable. End result: I got used to being invisible. I got used to giving and not receiving anything in return. To this day, I prefer to be in the background, and I can't handle compliments. I know that seems hard to believe, especially when you see how I carry myself. But it's the truth. I'm getting better, but it's still difficult.

6
THE EYE OF THE STORM

Sixteen was a difficult age for me. There was so much happening. So many changes were taking place, in all areas of my life. At this time, my mom was the director of a daycare center and went to school part time. "Xavier" was still being "Xavier". I was still having a difficult time with everything. I didn't fit in at home or school, and there were few people I could trust and confide in.

One day I went to my mom's job and there was a new employee, Lynette. Lynette was like no one I had ever met before. She was in her late 30s, early 40s and she was awesome! Full of energy and life, just an overall happy person. We instantly connected and I wanted to be around her all the time. She was such a giving and caring person, and she was such a wonderful mother. Now, it's not that my mother wasn't a good mother, but things were changing with our relationship. I desperately wanted the close relationship that we used to have. My mother was my best friend, my hero, my role model. But things were shifting. I started noticing things that I didn't like. Like the way she let "Xavier" call the shots, even when she knew he wasn't worthy. Lynette was everything that my mother wasn't. She had street smarts, and didn't take any mess. She was strong, confident, yet loving and giving. My mother was a very educated, goal-oriented, religious woman. So between the two, I had the perfect mother.

Lynette had a son, and boy was he fine! He was the same age, and had this thuggish edge about him that I found irresistible. Aside from that, he was so funny and we had a great time together. I remember the first time I stayed at Lynette's house, we spent the whole night in the car talking. I don't remember when we went in the house or when we fell asleep. All I know is that when I woke up, I was in his bed with my little sisters and he was at the foot of the bed, on top of the covers. That meant so much to me. He was the first guy that I encountered that didn't try to take advantage of me! Needless to say, I fell. Hard. From that day on, it was all about the two of us. I felt so safe and loved when I was with him.

My family spent so much time with Lynette's family, we were like one big happy family. Whenever we needed something, Lynette was there to help. One time in particular, we didn't have a car. Lynette let my mom drive one of her cars until we could afford one. That lady was an angel. I started calling her "Ma" and she didn't mind. She loved me like a daughter and she made sure everyone knew it. She would always say "no one understands our relationship." I confided in her, I trusted her. She knew about what was going on at home. Whenever things became unbearable, I was able to go to her house, no questions asked. Needless to say, they didn't care for my step dad too much, especially my boyfriend. He hated him with a passion.

My junior year, the unthinkable happened. It was a Monday in January. I remember because we had church the day before. I was home sick with "Xavier". I had the flu and my body was so weak. Now, let me just say, it had been a while since he touched me. It may have been the fact that I was always with Lynette and her family. Maybe it was because he had been preaching more, as a matter of fact, he had preached that Sunday. Or maybe he was lying low, like a snake in the grass. Either way, I thought the dark days were over. He and my mom were even getting along.

Anyway, that morning, "Xavier" had been studying the Bible. He called my mom to see if she was coming home for lunch because he was cooking. She declined because she had class. Now that I think of it, shouldn't he have known her schedule?

It's not like it had changed. Maybe he called to cover himself, or maybe it was a cry for help. Again, I'll never know.

"Xavier" gave me a dose of Nyquil and told me to go shower while lunch was cooking. Now let me back track for a minute. It was very rare that I took a shower if my little sister wasn't there to distract "Xavier". There was a time that he would use a mirror to look under the door when I showered. I actually told my mom, even showed her where the mirror was. She tested it to see if you could see anything under the door. Do you think she did anything to "Xavier"? Of course not. Do you think she tried to protect me in anyway? Of course not. So naturally, when "Xavier" told me to go shower, I hesitated. I remember sitting on my bed thinking something wasn't right. It felt weird. Even then I had the gift of discernment and didn't know it.

"Xavier" was in the hallway, vacuuming. He stopped at my door. I knew what was about to happen. Then I saw it, the mirror. I became so enraged! I had had enough. I swung open the door and told him that I was going to tell my mother. He said fine and went to get the phone. I stood there thinking *this is it. This ends today.* "Xavier" returned with the phone. When I went to reach for it, he grabbed me and threw me on my bed. It was so fast, like a scene from a movie. I couldn't believe what was happening. He stuck his hands down my pants. I was so scared I peed. I can still hear him whispering in my ear "I've been waiting so long for this." All I could do was cry and call on the name of Jesus. Suddenly, I felt this strength, it was a feeling I've never felt before. I punched him and we began to fight. I remember kicking and swinging. When I finally broke free, I ran down the hall and tried to reach the front door. He grabbed me and threw me on the floor. He got on top of me and demanded that I take off my shirt. We fought some more. I ran into the kitchen and grabbed a knife. I told him one of us wasn't going to make it out alive, the choice was his. That must have worked because he sat down and apologized. He actually tried to explain why he did it! I couldn't believe what was happening. According to him, he must have gotten his signals crossed, he thought I wanted him. I couldn't believe it. I remember saying "you are my daddy. How could you think I wanted you?" He looked at me with the saddest eyes I'd ever seen and then he opened the front door to let me go. I wasn't sure what his motive was, so I didn't move. He assured me that he wouldn't bother me anymore; he even gave me his ID and house key. I ran across the street to my neighbors' house. My face was covered with scratches and I was bleeding. When my neighbor opened the door, she immediately let me in and handed me the phone. I called my mom, but she didn't answer. I called the daycare and asked for Lynette. When she came to the phone, I began sobbing and asked that she come get me. When my mother finally returned to the daycare, I told her what happened. I don't know how I expected her to react, but her reaction was not what I expected. I can't explain the look on her face, but it was almost as if she didn't believe me. Or maybe she was in shock. All I know is that it wasn't what I expected. She didn't comfort me the way I thought she would. She didn't protect me the way I thought she would. To be honest, I don't think she held me or asked how I was doing. I remember my mom saying that we had to report it. I was relieved. I was like *ok, she believes me.* Her next words broke my heart. The only reason she wanted to report it was for her job security. According to her, if word got out about what happened and they knew she didn't report it, she could lose her job. Wow! That made me wonder, what if *she* had picked me up instead of Lynette. Would she have reported it? No one would've known. Like I mentioned before, it was no secret that "Xavier" and I had issues. This wasn't the first time something like this had happened. Now that I think about it, she *never* asked me how I felt after something happened. There was a time that "Xavier" and I got into an altercation and he punched me so hard that I couldn't lift my arm. My mom yelled at him for a brief second and then they had sex. She never came to ask me how I felt. My question wasn't answered until after I was married with children of my own, but for now, I was just relieved that it was over. Or so I thought....

7
DOWNPOUR

The events that followed that day were unreal. I had to undergo a series of rape kits and interviews. Every time I turned around, someone was asking me for a statement, picture, and sample. There was no peace. I felt so alone, so depressed, so violated. Even though there was no penetration, I felt like he had stolen my innocence, my life. It was worse than "Darrius", because this man was my parent. He watched me grow, he taught me things, and he loved me. Or did he? Was this love? Did love hurt? Maybe it did. Maybe this was all I was here for, a hollow shell meant to be used, mistreated and abused. I once believed God had called me. I knew that I was handpicked to do His will. Now I wasn't so sure. Surely the God I served wouldn't allow this to happen to me. Not me. Without knowing it, I was heading down a road of resentment that would take me places I never thought I would be.

My relationship between my mom and I really went south. I felt like she wasn't supportive. I guess she was dealing with her own demons, but at the time, I needed my mother and she wasn't there. In my mind, she made the situation about her; she always talked about how I treated her differently. How she didn't know what to do, she was hurt, etc. Not once (that I can recall) did she hold me and ask me how I felt. In an attempt to fix the situation, "Xavier's" mother set up a counseling session with one of her friends. This lady came to our house, this "minister." The whole time felt like a "let's beat down Javon" session. There we were, sitting in the living room. I was sitting on our old blue sofa with my mom and step grandma sitting on either side of me and the "minister" was sitting across from us in a chair. All I kept thinking about was the horror scene that took place in that very room not long before. I was reliving every detail. Being thrown on the floor, him sitting on top of me demanding that I take my clothes off. The longer I sat, the angrier I became. I really didn't want to relive that moment any more. I definitely didn't want to have this conversation in front of his mother and her friend. In my opinion, they had nothing to do with it.

My mom and step grandmother talked about how I was treating them differently, how they were hurt and felt like I blamed them. Once again, no one asked Javon how she felt.

No one held me, no one showed me what real love was supposed to feel like. They all sat there with the "woe is me" look on their faces. To make matters worse, the lady had the nerve to ask me what I did to provoke him. Did I lead him on? I had on a low cut t-shirt, which gave her more reason to pry. "Were you wearing something like you're wearing today?" That did it! That attitude that I had spent so much time perfecting was in full force. I didn't care about her title or who she thought she was. "Lady, I don't care if I was butt naked! That was my daddy and I was the child." I was so angry I could have slapped everyone in that room. It was clear that no one cared about me or my feelings. The old Javon was gone. I didn't want to hear about God, church, family, nothing. If no one else was going to look out for me, I would do it myself. By any means necessary.

When I finally returned to school, everything was different. I started skipping school to spend more time with my boyfriend. It began with me being late to class, to skipping class, to missing days all together. Up to this point, we never did anything but kiss. The more time we spent together, the more I knew I wanted to go there with him. This would be the first time I willingly gave myself to someone, and although I was nervous, I was ready. The way I looked at it, everyone else used my body for their own selfish pleasure, now it was my turn. At least I knew he loved me....

Even though I had turned a deaf ear to God, He was still speaking to me in subtle ways. I remember thinking that I was afraid to have sex, because once I started, I knew I wouldn't be able to stop. Needless to say, when I expressed this to my boyfriend, he wasn't very happy. Why would he be? I had all but promised him that I was going to take that next step with him and now I was going back on my word. Had I had the loving, nurturing relationship that a girl is supposed to have with her father, I would have seen the red flags. I would have known that this wasn't love. But that wasn't the case. I felt like I was going to lose him if I didn't fulfill my promise. So I did it. Surprisingly (or not, now that I think of it) it wasn't what I expected. I thought I was going to experience what I read about in all of my mom's Harlequin Romance novels. I just knew the earth was going to move and my boyfriend would declare his love and we would ride off into the sunset. Ha! Not even close. As a matter of fact, I saw the real him. He acted like it was nothing, like I was just another chick. He began disrespecting me and dating other girls in my face. But that didn't bother me, I was used to that kind of treatment. It was my normal, it was "love". So I was there. Whenever he needed me, despite how I felt about it. It wasn't like it was all bad; there were moments where he treated me the way he had in the beginning. Now looking back, I notice a pattern that I was oblivious to before. I would endure tons of pain, rejection and abuse just to get a glimpse of what appeared to be love.

8
AND... IT STARTS

As I thought, my encounter with my boyfriend opened a door that would take YEARS to close. I was in desperate search of love and affection and I would endure almost anything to have it. The crazy part is, when I actually came across anything that remotely resembled real love and respect, I pushed it away. It wasn't what I was used to and I didn't think I deserved it. This happened my senior year in high school.

When I began my senior year, I was a new person. I was no longer the same shy, Christian girl with little curves. Oh no! I was (in my mind) a mature young woman with the body and attitude to match. When I walked down the hall my first day, everyone noticed the change. A few boys even commented on it. You couldn't tell me NOTHING! All of the "popular" boys played on the football team and suddenly, they all wanted me. Except one. He and I were best friends and we talked about everything. It never occurred to me that he liked me, he was more like a brother. Every time a new guy tried to hit on me, I went to him. I even asked him to teach me to kiss, so the other guys wouldn't know how inexperienced I was. Now let's pause for a second, because I know you're probably thinking how could I not know how to kiss even though I was no longer "pure"? That was never something that I wanted to experience. I was always taught that kissing created a covenant, a commitment and I was saving that for marriage. I didn't realize that my body was just as precious. To me, my body had no value. It was something that everyone used for pleasure. But my mouth, that was sacred. It wasn't until recently that I realized just how valuable and priceless I really am, all of me.

In December of my senior year, I went away on a college tour, and all I could think about was my best friend and how I would be leaving him. That's when I realized I was in love with him. I couldn't wait to get back home to tell him! Imagine my relief when I found out he felt the same way! We immediately started dating and we were inseparable.

My boyfriend was a perfect gentleman. He never disrespected me or pressured me for sex. It was a wonderful relationship and I was in heaven. For a while. Eventually, I became bored. He was too nice, and we never argued. Ok, he never argued. I tried to find every reason to fight with him, but he wouldn't feed into it. He just wanted to talk it out. What?!?! That's not what I was used to. I wanted him to yell at me, ignore me, cheat on me, but he never did.

During this time, I started working at the mall. There was this guy that worked at the store next to where I worked. He would always come by my store to flirt and talk. Although he wasn't the cutest, I loved his sense of humor. I also loved the fact that he was an older guy with this thuggish edge that I found irresistible. We exchanged numbers and we began a relationship.

The next few months were like a rollercoaster. One minute I was head over heels for my boyfriend, the next it was all about the "thug". In October of 2004, I found out I was pregnant. During this time, I had been with only my boyfriend for quite some time, so we knew the baby was his. I've always been an honest person, so he knew about the other guy. He still wanted to be my side the entire way. July 23, 2005 we welcomed Malik Archibald into the world and it was one of the greatest moments in my life.

My boyfriend was the perfect dad. He was there for everything. Whatever we needed, he supplied. At that time, it became common knowledge that I was messing with two people at the same time and his family did not agree. We were constantly arguing about what his mother had heard or what they thought they knew. Although I knew who the baby belonged to, I didn't want to ruin his life so I lied. I told him that the baby wasn't his. He had an opportunity to go to college and I didn't want to stop him. In my own way, I loved him and I thought I was doing what was best. I was young, I didn't know any better. Plus I had my mother in my ear. She was always asking me was I sure and telling me how I was causing him so many problems. So we broke up. He went away to college and I was left to take care of my baby on my own.

After my boyfriend left, I felt lost. My mom and sisters really stepped up to help with Malik. We were spending so much time together and it was really pleasant. I even became active in church again. One of "Darrius"' brothers had started a church and my mom was a member. At first, I was hesitant to trust anyone in the church, especially knowing the history. When we got there, everyone seemed to be really open and loving. No one mentioned what had occurred years ago and I was ecstatic. I became active in the church; I even began praise dancing again. The happiness didn't last. Some of the members began treating my sisters and me differently. They were always talking about our attitudes or how disrespectful we were. As usual, some of the men in the church were flirting with me. This one man even stuck his hand down my shirt in church!

One day, "Darrius" came and performed at the church and we started talking. He wanted me to join his dance group again. I told him that I needed to think about it and he said we should get together and talk. The next day, he came and picked me up and we went to the park. He brought a few of his other dancers as well.

When we got to the park, he told the two girls to get out of the car. They weren't too far away so I knew I would be safe. He began talking about how he couldn't believe I was a mother and I had grown into such a beautiful young lady. Next he started talking about everything that he went through after we left the church when I was younger. According to him, his wife left him and took her kids. He also said his career suffered, no one wanted him to perform at his church. He couldn't understand why I wanted to hurt him so badly, when all he wanted to do was love me. He said he had been in love with me since I was a little girl and he was only trying to show his love. He even began crying. Although I was a "grown" woman, I felt like a little girl all over again. It hurt me to see him cry like that. I felt guilty. I thought *what have I done? Maybe he really did love me.* He begged me to join his dance crew. He said he needed me. He agreed to meet with my mom to apologize and let her know everything was ok. He met with my mom and I joined the crew.

I loved being back with the crew. Most of the people that I performed with as a child were still members and it was like a family reunion. We always had a good time and they all loved Malik. We would go there almost every day. "Darrius" never did anything to disrespect me and he gave me all of the lead parts. It was like nothing had ever happened.

One day we were in the studio working on my solo part on his latest song. My head wasn't on the music and I kept messing up. He sent everyone out of the room so we could talk. I don't remember what all he said, but at the end of his speech, he asked me did I have his back. Of course I said yes and I apologized for messing up. He hugged me and told me everything would be ok. Then he did it. He kissed me. I remember looking at him like I had seen a ghost. I was frozen in that moment. He asked me if that was ok and if not to give him the hand. I slowly lifted my hand, but the rest of my body was still stuck. He laughed and kissed me again. I didn't know what to do. He kept repeating "I love you Javon. You're a woman now. We can be together. I love you." He said it would have to be our secret because no one would understand. He said we would hurt his wife and kids. I didn't want to do that, I loved them. So I didn't say anything.

After that night, he was unstoppable. It was like I was reliving my childhood all over again. He would find reasons to be alone with me so he could kiss me. Although I didn't like it, I felt like I couldn't do anything. I had a baby so people knew I was active. Besides, I was an adult now. I had the power to stop him if I wanted to. But I didn't. People would think that I wanted it, and that I lied back when I was a child. So I dealt with it.

One day he came to the house and I was home alone. He said he couldn't stop thinking about me and he had to see me. One minute we were on the couch talking and the next thing I knew, we were on the floor and he was pulling off my pants. I remember trying to stop him and shaking my head no. This was going too far. I tried to tell him that my sisters would be home soon but that didn't stop him. He asked me if I loved him because he loved me. I laid there looking at him for what seemed like forever. He looked so vulnerable. I felt like he really loved me. This was all I knew. Sex equaled love. I loved him, and although it wasn't in the way he meant it, I didn't want to disappoint him. So I gave him my body.

We began having sex on a regular basis. I was so confused. I hated what we were doing, but I loved the attention he gave me. He was always checking on me and he was there anytime I needed something. Once again, I found myself in a state of depression. Once again, I blamed God. I always prayed about the situation, but it seemed like nothing changed. I tried cutting back how much I communicated with him, but he would show up at my door. I started dating a guy in the crew and I spent all of my time with him. Needless to say, "Darrius" did not like that at all. He was always giving us evil looks at rehearsal.

One night after rehearsal, he came to my house. When I opened the door, he immediately embraced me. "Let's go, let's go tell my wife I'm in love with you and I want to be with you." I thought he was insane. What was he thinking? I told him that there was no way that I could be with him. He asked if I loved him and I said yes but not in the way he thought. I explained that I was seeing the guy in the crew and I was happy. I told him that what we were doing was wrong and we had to stop. He looked at me with the saddest eyes I'd ever seen. He kissed me and headed towards the door. Before he left, he said "I guess I was only dreaming. If so, I don't want to wake up." The next day we went to the studio for rehearsal. He explained to the crew that he had been up all night writing a new song. The title? I'm Only Dreaming. It was too much to deal with. I left the crew that day.

9
INTRODUCING JEWLZ

In April 2006, I was sitting in my mother's room talking to my mom and my best friend about how I needed a job. I was getting benefits from social services, but it wasn't enough to take care of my bills and my mother's. Contrary to what she says, I was still taking care of her and my sisters. Don't get me wrong, she had a job, but she always needed help. It was my job to make sure they were ok. It was always my job.

I was reading the paper when I saw an ad for a waitress in a strip club, making $1000 a week. We started joking about me applying. I mean, I worked at Hooter's for a few months, so this couldn't have been any worse. I don't remember exactly how the conversation went, but the end result was me applying for the job the next day, with my mother's approval. I was hired on the spot and began work the following weekend. On my first day, I remember my mom saying "how much do you think you're going to make, cuz we have a light bill due." That night I brought home $11 dollars, which was nowhere near enough, so I started dancing.

My mom and I picked out an outfit and my best friend sat with me at work that night. When we got to the club, the manager walked me through how everything worked and introduced me to the bouncers and the DJ. Although it wasn't my first time in the club, it felt different. The atmosphere felt different. I was so nervous, so scared. I felt like a little girl all over again. The manager asked me what my name would be, and it occurred to me that I never thought about it. He made suggestions like Cinnamon, Candy, Diamond, but they all sounded so stripper like. I wanted to be different. After careful thought, I came up with Jewlz. He looked at me with this look that I couldn't understand. I explained "some girls are a diamond, others may be a pearl, and some may even be gold. But me, I'm everything wrapped in one. I'm Jewlz." He flossed this sly, cocky grin and I knew that we would make money together. I sat with my friend the whole night, drinking and thinking, trying to get my nerves up. When I heard the DJ announce that I was next, I quickly guzzled my lemon drop and headed to the back. I stood in the mirror staring at myself, wondering how I gotten to that point. How did the girl that loved God so much, singing and dancing in churches all over town, end up here? The girl who gave her life to God at 6, accepted the call a few years later, and preached all over the East coast. Then I thought about how that same God had allowed so much to happen to that girl, and suddenly it no longer mattered. This was my reality and I was ready to own it. I walked on stage, confidant and free. The music started and I began to move in ways that I didn't know I had. I wasn't like the other girls that I had seen popping and dropping all over stage. No. I moved slowly and seductively. I was in control and I loved it. To be on stage, touching and caressing myself, knowing that the men wanted to but couldn't, gave me a feeling that I had never felt before. Finally, *I* was in charge of what happened to my body. *I* was in control of my feelings, who touched me, and how my body reacted. The walls were lined with floor to ceiling mirrors. I caught a glimpse of myself standing there, with all those men staring up at me. I was *beautiful, sexy, and powerful.* It was a high that I had never felt and I quickly became addicted.

Jewlz was everything that I wasn't and without realizing it, I developed a double life. During the day, I was a loving young mother that cared for her son, mother and sisters. I still lived at home and followed every rule that my mother set for me, even though I made majority of the money and paid the majority of the bills. I never questioned her authority and I never had a say in what I did or where I went. There were days she would take my money that I earned, and I never said a word. My mother had a way of intimidating me and making me feel like I owed her something.

At night, I was Jewlz. Free, sexy and in charge. Every night was a constant party and I partied HARD. Alcohol was available to me in large quantities, even though I was only 20. I never had a problem standing up for myself, in fact, I was quite the bully. I was always starting trouble and getting into fights. It was nothing for me to smash a girl's head in the mirror or hit her with my stiletto. Looking back at it now, it was nothing but God's grace and mercy that kept me, because I should have been in jail or worse. And my attitude... ugh! I was so conceited it was sickening. I knew I was the hottest thing in the club and everyone else knew it too. While everyone else had weave down their back with their fake *everythings* covered in makeup, I was all natural and wore very little makeup. I had songs that were designated just for me and the DJ even made a custom introduction: "Coming to the stage, shining like a diamond, it's Jewlz!" When the manager had the idea to do shower shows on stage, I was the first to volunteer. It was a huge success and I made tons of money. The night life was great!

Things got so bad at home that I became tired of living the double life. My mom and I were constantly arguing and she was always finding reasons to take my money. I felt as if she was taking advantage of me. It was like the more I made, the more she took. I began writing down my income on a calendar to track my savings as well as pay my tithes. Proverbs 22:6 says *"Train up a child in the way he should go: and when he is old, he will not depart from it (KJV)."* Even though I was living a life of sin, I still had enough sense to pay my tithes. One day my mom saw the calendar and made a comment that I should have more to show for my money. I was thinking, *are you serious?!?* There would be times that money would come up missing from my room and no one knew where it went. Around this time, she had also begun visiting "Xavier" in prison. I hated being Javon. The only thing I enjoyed was Malik. He gave me a sense of love and hope that I had never experienced and I made sure he had everything he needed, including a loving mother. No matter how late I stayed out or how drunk I was, I never neglected my baby. He kept me sane, so many times. He was my lifeline.

I began spending as much time as Jewlz as I could. I would go into work at 4 pm and stay until we closed at 3am. I barely took a day off, maybe once every few weeks. During this time I started "dating" the manager of the club. We spent a lot of time together. When we were weren't working, we were at his house. One day we talked about my dreams and goals and I realized that I wanted to go back to school. Although things were crazy at that time, I wanted a better life for my son. I enrolled myself in school the next day. My plan was to dance my way through school, that way I could still take care of my son. After I graduated, I would be done forever. Although a lot of people disagreed with my choices, I was proud of myself. I was taking care of myself and my son, and I put myself back in school. No one could say they gave me anything.

The only time I was home was when I knew my mom wasn't. One day we got into an argument and she left a letter on my dresser. The letter basically said I acted like the world owed me something and she was sick of it. She wanted me to move out. It was ironic that it came at a time that "Xavier" was getting out of prison. My mom had already mentioned several times before that they were getting back together. According to her, God had shown her that they were meant to be family and I was going to be ok with it. There it was again, "God" was making decisions for my life that I couldn't control. It didn't occur to me that maybe God had nothing to do with it, perhaps it was just human nature. All I knew was that once again, I was hurting and God didn't help me. I moved out of my mom's house and stayed with Lynette.

Around this time, Myspace was very popular. I met this guy and we began chatting. He seemed like someone I wanted to know. We talked at least twice a day. One day he asked me to come visit him (he lived about two hours away). After that first day, I was in love. I started to visit him every chance I got. He was perfect. He was thuggish (of course) but he was a perfect gentleman and he loved my son. We talked about everything, our dreams our goals, our past. He even got me to return to church. Eventually I moved in with him. That's when his true colors came out.

10
PAIN

When I first moved in with my boyfriend, it was like a dream. I was so happy. There we were, a cute little family, in this double wide trailer that we shared with his best friend and his mother. To make the dream complete, we had a huge yard and several dogs. Everyone loved Malik like he was their own, and I even got along with his mother. I was so happy that I put Jewlz on the back burner and focused on Javon, The Housewife. I did it all, cooked, cleaned, even laid out his clothes and ran his bath water. After a few months, I left the club and got a job in a daycare. My future was looking bright.

Eventually reality set in. His mother began taking my things out of our bedroom without asking and always made comments about it being her house. He never defended me, which would cause an argument. When we argued, he would get so angry. He always threatened to put me "6ft under." It was horrible. When the yelling didn't satisfy him anymore, he became physically abusive. Who was this person? This wasn't the person I fell in love with. I didn't realize that this was the real him, I just fell in love with his representative.

Without realizing it, I was losing myself. I became so intimated by everyone in the house, I would lock myself in the room. I also found out that my boyfriend was cheating on me with his ex. I was so depressed. Once in a while, we would have a good day and I would become hopeful that things could change, but they never did. No matter how much we fought, they never mistreated Malik and I wanted him to have a dad. So I stayed.

One day, his mom called me in her room. Her and his aunt were in there getting high on marijuana. She asked me why I didn't smoke. This wasn't the first time we had this conversation. Everyone in the house smoked, and they thought it was so strange that I didn't. She told me that getting high would calm me down and would make everyone get along better. She even said that my boyfriend liked women who smoked and that's why he went back to his ex. Needless to say, I got high. We actually had a great night, laughing and joking. I was relieved. After that I was always smoking with the family, it bonded us.

That lasted for a while, but eventually things went back to

normal. I was the only one in the house with a legitimate job and bills were piling up. One day I came home from work and the lights were off. I couldn't let my baby live in a house with no lights, so I went back to the one thing I knew would provide, Jewlz. I would work at the daycare during the week and the club on the weekend.

My boyfriend loved the fact that I was bringing in money and I loved the fact that I was able to get away every weekend. That was my freedom, my time to let my hair down. When I was Jewlz, I felt loved and I had no problem standing up for myself. I fought more than I had before. I partied harder than I had before. I was spinning out of control. I even began sleeping with some of my customers. Now that I look back, I understand that I was a classy prostitute. No I wasn't standing on the corner waiting on men to pick me up, but it was just as bad. Let me make something clear for every woman reading this book. If you are giving a man your body and all you get in return is money and gifts, you're prostituting yourself. Point blank, period, end of discussion. No matter what you say or what you call it, that's the truth. There's no honor in that, it's not cute, and it will get you nowhere. I know that now. Back then, I just thought I was irresistible and could have any man I wanted. I knew my boyfriend was cheating so I was getting back at him. I didn't realize that I was only hurting myself.

During this time, I started talking to my mother again although we didn't see each other very often. I would stay at her house while I was in town for the weekend. When she wasn't there, she and my sisters were visiting "Xavier". They spent a lot of time together. She was still convinced that they were getting back together and she was trying to get me on board. She was always talking about how much he changed, how he was back in church, etc. All I could think about was what he did to me and how my mother was choosing him over me. I couldn't see how anyone would want to be with someone who attacked their child. I would kill over my child. Every time we tried to talk about it, she would find a way to bring up God, but I didn't want to hear it. By this time, I was a little over God and His decisions. Clearly we weren't on the same page. I was filled with so much anger and hatred. For God, my family, my boyfriend, everyone. I was numb and my heart had turned cold towards everything.

One day, I came home from work and my boyfriend was going through my stuff. He found some jewelry that I had been hiding. When he questioned me about it, I told him the truth about what I had been doing. I wanted to hurt him, I wanted him to feel what I felt when I found out he was cheating on me. I thought he would realize how much he loved me and he would straighten up, but that's not what happened. He punched me so hard I fell against the wall. I was so shocked! I didn't have time to process what happened because before I knew it, he had me in the air choking the life out of me. I remember hearing Malik crying and that was it! I grabbed him by his dreads and yanked them until he let me go. I don't think he expected it because he stared at me like he had seen a ghost. But I wasn't through. I slapped him so hard his head spun. After that it was WW3. Finally his mom broke it up and I grabbed my son and left. I didn't know where I was going. My mom was not an option and I didn't have money for a hotel. I called my boss to tell her that I wouldn't be at work the next day. When she asked for an explanation, I broke down. She told me to stay with her. I couldn't believe it. Outside of work, we knew nothing about each other, yet she opened her home to me. She and her husband treated me and Malik like her own flesh and blood and we stayed with her for a few months. When I announced that we were going back to my boyfriend's, she was devastated. She begged me not to go. The Bible says warning comes before destruction. God was trying to save me, but I didn't pay attention. I went back to my boyfriend and it was one of the worst decisions of my life.

My boyfriend and I began fighting so much that if a day went by that we didn't, I thought something was wrong. He was always calling me outside of my name and telling me he would kill me. It was so bad that Malik began yelling and hitting people. This wasn't the life that I imagined, but I didn't want to leave him. Even though we were going through all of that, I loved him. I would make excuses for our fights: his father left him, I upset him, he's unhappy with himself. No matter what, I felt like he gave me a place to stay and he was a dad to my son. He had to love me and if I worked on it, eventually he would realize how much he hurt me and he would change.

A friend of mine recently preached a message about pain. He said pain was a part of life, you can't avoid it. There will always be pain, whether unnecessary or necessary. My time with my boyfriend was unnecessary pain. I chose to be in that position. I made the decision to move in with him and I made the decision to stay. That decision almost killed me, broke me down to nothing. One day I found out I was pregnant. I couldn't bring a child into that mess. So I did the only thing I thought I could do, I terminated the pregnancy. It was the worst thing I could've done. I didn't believe in abortion, but what else could I do? I was so depressed I no longer had the will to live, not even for my son. I began telling myself that he would be better off without me. I wanted to die so he could have a better life. A few days later, I was home alone, I don't remember where everyone was. I sat in my bedroom staring at the walls. In an effort to calm down, I smoked a blunt. When that didn't work, I called my grandma and she immediately knew something was wrong. She started praying and speaking life, but I didn't want to receive it. Tears ran down my face as I tried to tell her that I wasn't in the mood for prayer, but she wouldn't listen. She continued to speak life into me. She told me I had purpose, I was anointed and a great mother. She said I was strong, smart and beautiful. I remember thinking that she was only saying that because she didn't know what was really going on. When we got off the phone I wrote two letters; one to Malik and one to my grandma. I took several pills, and waited to die. The next thing I remember, I was on the floor shaking and my boyfriend was yelling my name. I was rushed to the emergency room. When we got to the hospital, the Dr. asked what I had taken. The last thing I remember was closing my eyes as tears ran down my face, thinking *let me die*.

After that, my mom called my Aunt and asked her if I could move in with her. I didn't tell my mom exactly what happened that last day, but she knew we were fighting a lot and she wanted to get me and her grandson as far away from that place as she could. My Aunt agreed and I moved to Maryland.

When I first got to Maryland, I had mixed emotions. I was excited about leaving my ex and being back with my Aunt, but

I wasn't too excited about living in a house with my Uncle and little cousins. They had too many rules and I never had any privacy. I had to sneak to get high, but I'm sure my family knew something was wrong. I was a mess. My attitude was scary, my wardrobe was trashy and my mouth was reckless. No matter what, my aunt and uncle were so patient with me. They constantly reminded me that they loved and supported me, no matter how much I resented them.

My aunt always took me with her wherever she went and made sure I was around positive women. She showed me a different way of life. Here were these strong, beautiful women and they all loved and provided for their children. They were career women, God-fearing women. They demanded respect and they gave it in return. They were in control of their lives and didn't use their bodies to get there. I wanted some of that. I found a job working in a corporate office and I began going back to church. I started smoking less and less and I even registered for school. For the first time in a long time, life seemed bearable.

The church that I went to was completely different from any church that I had ever attended. For starters, the pastor was a female. But it was more to it. Her message was so real, so down to earth. She broke the Word down and made it applicable to real, modern day life. Watching her made me realize that I missed the feeling that I felt when I shared God's word. I wasn't ready to jump back in the pulpit, but I was ready to hear His voice. I knew it would be a slow process, but for the first time, I was willing. It was through my studies that I began to see some of my issues and I realized that I needed help. I even reconnected with my mother.

As the days went on, I became happier and happier, but something was missing. I missed being in a relationship. Of course I had the love of my family and friends, but I felt like I needed love from a man. My man. I reconnected with my ex and we began dating again. Against the advice of my Aunt, I went to visit him every chance I got. I even sent him money to help with his bills. We were in love. We were going to get married and be a family. He even agreed to go to church with me!

One day, I went to visit him, but this time was different. He didn't want me to meet him at his house. He said he wanted to make it special so we went to a hotel. While we were there, his phone kept ringing, but he never answered it. I thought it was strange and when I questioned him about it, he said it was because he didn't want us to be interrupted. I was in love, so I believed him. When we got back to his house, I went inside to say good bye to his mom and that's when I saw a letter addressed to his ex! I couldn't believe my eyes. It was then that I realized the toys around the house. I went into his room and I couldn't believe my eyes. Her things were everywhere. I was sending him money and he was living with another woman. At that moment, I declared that I would never be in that situation again. A man would never get anything else from me, not even a stick of gum. And definitely not my heart. Of course, I found a reason to blame God. I felt like once again I was trying to live right and once again, it failed. I was over this new life and Maryland. My mom talked me into moving back home with her. She said we could get a bigger place and they would be there to help with Malik. I jumped at the opportunity.

11
THE PROCESS

One thing I have learned, when God takes you out of something or removes something or someone out of your life, leave it alone. It may not be easy, but you have to fight to keep what God has done. Too many times, God answers our prayers and does what is best for us, but because it may be uncomfortable or new, we go back to what we know. Let me give you another example. Take someone that has been incarcerated for several years. While they are locked up, they dream about getting out, even make plans for the day they are released. When they get out, everything is different. They realize that they need to work to have what they need. People may not treat them nice because of their past. They start realizing what it's like on the outside and they become depressed. They realize that being locked up, they had a guaranteed bed and three meals a day. Eventually they return to the same things that caused them to get locked up in the first place. At least in prison, they know what to expect and it's easier. It's comfortable. I didn't realize that I was in prison and Maryland was my way of escape. All I knew was that it wasn't what I was used to; it was uncomfortable. I once heard someone say that comfort and growth cannot coexist. I now understand what that means.

When I moved back to North Carolina, it was as if Maryland never existed. At this time I was living with my mom again. Although she thought things were fine between us, I couldn't get over the fact that she and my sisters were still spending so much time with "Xavier". They were acting like a real family. To avoid the pain that I was experiencing, I went back to the club, back to the drugs and alcohol. Malik was always with my mom and my sisters, so I had a lot of time to self-destruct. As long as I was high, I didn't think about the things that were hurting Javon. I didn't want to face my reality, I didn't want to face my pain. The fantasy world of Jewlz was better. Jewlz didn't have problems. She could get into any club for free and everyone loved her. The people that didn't love her were afraid of her, so they didn't bother her. Jewlz was in control and Javon was dying slowly, both naturally and spiritually.

In March of 2008, I was in a terrible car accident. I was spending the day with my two little sisters and Malik. In true

Jewlz fashion, I was speeding down the highway with my music blasting. I thought I was so cute. I came to a stop sign but instead of stopping, I tried to make a left turn before the oncoming cars passed me. My car was hit on the driver side and I fractured my pelvis. The car was totaled but I was the only person injured. I was put on crutches and told to stay out of work for a month. I don't know if that was a wakeup call from God or an attempt to take my life. Either way, I ignored the signs. I doped myself up on the prescribed pain pills and returned to work after two weeks.

The first night that I went back to work, I was in so much pain that I began popping pills like skittles. After a while, I was numb to the pain and reality. I was back to my old self, drinking, partying and making money. It was a high like nothing I'd ever experienced and I loved it. Without realizing it, I was developing an addiction to prescription pain pills. I was taking way more than I was prescribed and when those ran out, I found pills from people I knew. Money wasn't an issue, and before I knew it I was spending close to $80 a day on pills. I was a functioning addict so no one knew anything was wrong. I didn't even think anything was wrong. I've seen movies about people who become strung out on drugs and they lose their minds. They isolate themselves from everyone and begin doing anything for that high. That wasn't me. I still went to church, spent time with my family and took care of my son; I thought I was fine. At work, I was surrounded by other addicts. Girls were constantly sharing drugs with each other. I began experimenting with different pills, many times without knowing what they were. My life was once again spinning out of control.

There was a girl at the club and we became good friends. We were total opposites, but there was something about her that attracted me. I had feelings that I never felt for anyone before, especially not a woman. We did everything together. She was my listening ear, my shoulder to cry on, my escape from reality. She introduced me to a world that I didn't know existed. At work we were the dynamic duo. We were both known for our dancing skills and we began doing sets together. It's a well-known fact that girl-on-girl action is popular in a strip club. Because we were friends I felt comfortable with her. One night we did a shower show together. One thing led to another and before I knew it, we were making out on stage. After that we began dating. Never in a million years did I think I would ever kiss a girl, let alone be in a relationship with one. I felt like I had gone so far from grace that nothing would make a difference. As far as I was concerned, God was nowhere near me so as long as I thought I was happy, I did whatever I felt like doing.

She and I dated for about three months. We were inseparable. I felt like she loved and understood me better than anyone had ever done and I wanted to do whatever I had to in order to keep her around. I thought she was perfect. Until I found out she was cheating on me. I was devastated. I kept wondering what was wrong with me. Was I not worthy of love? Would I ever be happy? A few months later, she came back and said she wanted to be with me. Because I wanted to be loved, I took her back. Not long after that, we broke up again. It was like a light bulb went off. I was like Javon, what are you doing. It's bad enough that you're being played, but to be played by a woman? I needed to take a break from the club for a while. I needed to get back to what was important. Me and my baby. I moved back in with Lynette and found a job working as a community support worker. It was a rough transition, and I still got high from time to time, but I was determined to make a better life for my son. I even started going back to church with my mom and sisters. She and "Xavier" had divorced and he had married someone else. I thought there was hope.

12
PRESSURE

One Sunday after church, my mom and I were in the kitchen cooking dinner. We were having a conversation about the church service. For the first time in a long time, I felt God's presence and it was a great experience. I knew that I had been delivered from my sins and I was ready to move forward in Him. My mom began talking about how she was also delivered from some things. I was used to it by now, she always has a way of turning the conversation on her. It didn't matter, I was still on cloud nine. The conversation quickly went south. I remember it like it was yesterday. I was at the sink rinsing macaroni noodles when I heard my mom say "there was a time that I hated you and was jealous of you." I froze. You know how in the movies when something shocking happens, the music stops and everything goes quiet? Yeah it was one of those moments. When I didn't say anything, she continued. "I mean, you know how when your man cheats, you hate the other woman? Well in this case, you were the other woman." I stood there, speechless. I wasn't the other woman. I was the child and he was an adult. Not just any adult, my parent. Why couldn't anyone see what I was going through? Did no one care about Javon at all? How could God allow this to happen to me, especially after the encounter we just had a few hours ago? I remember trying to explain my feelings to my mother. She brushed them off by saying that she was over it now so it didn't matter. We finished cooking dinner as if nothing had happened, but inside I was falling apart. I felt so unloved, so misunderstood. Once again, I questioned my purpose in the world. Nothing that I did mattered to anyone. I felt like no one would miss me if I disappeared. When I got back to Lynette, I told her what happened. I couldn't hold it in any longer. I told her I felt like I was losing my mind. She encouraged me to seek help. I contacted a counseling service immediately.

My first session was weird. I spent most of the time talking about how I didn't believe in letting my feelings show. I felt like talking to her would be a waste of time. Either she was going to tell me I was crazy and take my child or she would brush it off and tell me that I was overreacting. Either way, I was not eager about opening up. After a few more sessions, I began to open up more and it was really helpful. I liked it because it wasn't faith-based. Not that I had anything against Christian counselors, but I needed to hear real answers to my real life questions. I didn't want to be told to just pray and trust that everything would be ok. Through my sessions, I was able to see how my childhood had impacted my adult life. Survivors of childhood sexual abuse react in one of two ways; either they hate sex and intimacy all together or they are very loose with their sexuality. It isn't uncommon for victims to begin sexual relationships with their abusers when they become adults. I realized how my search for love and value was causing me to allow people to use me in every area of my life. The reality was too much to face. Once I began seeing all of my issues, I panicked. I felt like I was so messed up, and there was no way to fix me. I stopped going to my sessions and turned back to the one thing I knew would make me feel better: Jewlz. I worked at the club on the weekends. During the day, I went to work as a community support worker. Imagine trying to help people when you're falling apart inside. I was a mess.

One day I was in the office getting my assignment for the next day. The owner pulled me in her office to talk. She said she noticed a change in me and wanted to know if everything was ok. I broke down and told her everything; about my mom, my job as a dancer, my suicidal thoughts. She listened to my rant for what seemed like hours. When I was done, she asked if she could help. She wanted to take Malik while I got myself together. The idea seemed like a good one. She was a Christian African American woman, married with several kids of her own. She assured me that Malik would be well taken care of and I could see and talk to him whenever I needed to. She could give him everything that I couldn't and I could get myself together. Although I didn't want to give up my baby, I knew that I was not in the place to give what he needed and deserved. I went and gathered him and his belongings and met her at the office. When they pulled off, I sat in the parking lot for hours crying.

When I got home, Lynette asked where Malik was. She was not happy with what I had done and she immediately called my mom. My mom couldn't believe what I had done. She wanted to know why I would give my child up. According to my mom, she didn't think things were that bad and she wanted Malik. I lost it! Why would I give my child to her? She was the main reason I was screwed up. I began crying and telling everything that I had been dealing with, everything that I had been holding inside since high school. Once again, she never acknowledged what I did. She made the conversation about her, how I blamed her, I hated her and nothing she did was good enough. I couldn't take anymore. I hung up the phone. I thought it was over, but I was wrong. She called my boss consistently, asking her to bring Malik to her. Of course my boss denied. Lynette said that if I didn't bring Malik home, I would have to find somewhere else to live. I felt like I was doing what was best for him, but no one saw it that way. All they saw was that I had given him away. I went and got Malik the next day. When I brought him home, Lynette hugged me and said that she did it for me, not him. She knew that if I didn't have him I would've died. And she was right.

The next year consisted of a lot of self-medicating. I did everything I could to numb the pain. I didn't care about anyone other than my son, not even myself. I only looked in the mirror long enough to do my makeup. On the outside, I was gorgeous. On the inside, I was dark, ugly, cold, dead. I began sleeping with people just because I could. To me, my body didn't have a value, I was only here as a sexual object. I used it to get whatever and whoever I wanted. In May of 2009, I found out I was pregnant which was the last thing I needed. There was no way I could have that baby. I wasn't capable of taking care of it and the father was not someone that I could have a baby with. Once again, I was faced with a painful decision. I did the only thing that I thought I could, I terminated another pregnancy. It was the scariest thing I have ever experienced, even worse than the first time. I had waited too long to get the procedure done so it was very painful and very risky. I remember laying on the chair staring at the ceiling with tears in my eyes. When I heard the vacuum, I didn't know what to think. I was so scared. The doctor told me to start counting, as if that was supposed to take my mind off of what was happening. All I could think about was the fact that I was killing another baby. The pain was like nothing I had ever experienced and because I was so far along, it took longer than normal. I felt like I was going to die. On the way back home, I got so sick. I mean really sick. I just knew I was dying. When I got home, all I could do was lay in the bed and cry for days. I can't explain how I felt, but it was the wake-up call that I needed. I vowed to never terminate another pregnancy again. I also decided at that moment that I was going to change my life and be a better mother to Malik.

13
STABILITY

Shortly after that, I moved into my first apartment. It was a small one bedroom apartment and we moved in with nothing but our clothes, a full-size bed, and a small TV. Our first night was the most peaceful night we had ever experienced. When I woke up the next morning, I was so happy. I spent the whole day with my son, and it is a memory that I will always cherish. I wanted to spend more time with him, so I cut down how much I worked at the club. It was no longer an escape, it was a job. I worked just enough to cover my bills. My son was my happiness.

About a month after I moved in, my mom was having financial troubles and her lights were turned off. She asked if she could stay with me until she received her next pay check. Although we still had a rocky relationship, I still felt like it was my duty to help her and my sisters, so I let them move in. Two weeks turned into four and the next thing I knew she was talking about letting go of her apartment and moving in with me. She never asked how I felt, she just told me that she was going to do it. I felt like I didn't have a say in what went on in my house. It began to feel like her house and I was living there. It was like history was repeating itself. She didn't help with any bills and they barely contributed around the house. After a while, I didn't want to go home and went back to working seven nights a week, just to get a break. I became irritated with any and everything and I was always getting into fights at work.

One night while I was on stage, I noticed this man pointing and smiling at me. No matter where I went, his eyes followed me. Even after I got off stage, I noticed him staring at me across the room. I didn't think much of it, I was used to that kind of behavior. Thinking I could turn him into a regular, I went to talk to him. Immediately, I noticed something different about him. He was actually interested in me as a person. He asked me my name and without hesitation, I said Javon. In all my years as a dancer, I had never given anyone my real name. Not even the girls that I worked with knew my name, everyone called me Jewlz. I spent the entire night talking to him. I only made a total of $21 that night, all from him. Before he left, we exchanged numbers and he called me once he got home. We talked all night and again the next day. I really enjoyed his conversation and he was such a gentleman. We started spending a lot of time together and very quickly, I fell in love. He was everything that I was looking for, and nothing like anyone I had ever dated. We talked about everything. He knew my past and understood that I wasn't that person anymore. He never judged anything that I told him, he just held me and talked through it. He always assured me that everything would be ok. I introduced him to my family after two months of dating and two months after that, we were engaged. I was happier than I had ever been in my life. I was finally going to be able to give Malik the life that he deserved, the life that I never had. I realized that the first thing I had to do was address the major issues in my life. By this time my mom had moved out and was living in her own apartment. I went to visit her one day in the hopes to have a serious heart to heart about the issues that I was facing. Immediately, she became defensive and the conversation began to turn negative. Realizing that it was going nowhere, I changed the subject and decided to address "Xavier". I wrote him a letter and explained how he had affected my life. I also told him that I loved him and I forgave him for everything. I knew if I didn't address my demons, they would follow me into the next phase of my life. After that, I felt like a weight had been lifted. I rededicated my life to God and was ready for my future.

The honey moon phase quickly vanished and reality set it. My fiancé lost his job and I had to return to work. Because he was going to school during the day, I went back to the club and he stayed with Malik at night. I hated working at the club, it wasn't like before. Money was slow, and eventually we lost our apartment and had to move in with my mom. Although we only stayed with her for two weeks, it was the longest two weeks of my life. We argued a lot and my mother was constantly interfering in our relationship. She even told him lies to convince him that I was cheating. Eventually we called off the engagement, until I found out I was pregnant. Although I knew we weren't happy, I didn't want to have another baby out of wedlock and abortion was out of the question. So we decided to get married.

I hate to say that my pregnancy was one of the worst periods of my life, but it was. It wasn't that I wasn't happy about the baby, I wasn't happy with the status of our relationship. We were constantly fighting and we never had enough money. I had to return to the club for the first three months of my pregnancy. After that, I worked as a bartender in a downtown bar. The further I got in my pregnancy, the more it affected my pelvis and back from the previous car accident. I was in so much pain, but because of my previous addiction to pills, I refused to be put on medication. My fiancé had to do everything around the house. I couldn't even walk without my pelvic bone popping. I also put on a lot of weight and couldn't fit anything in my closet. My self-esteem was so low. I knew that I was no longer the sexy Jewlz that my fiancé had fallen in love with, I didn't even have the same figure. I felt so ugly, so useless. I became depressed and eventually, I began letting myself go. My fiancé started spending more time away from the house and it was obvious that he was finding comfort somewhere else. Because I never had "proof" I didn't say anything about it. We were married in November 2010 and had our son, Cambrin Arnez, a month later.

Before two people decide to get married, they should know everything about each other; their likes and dislikes, their parenting styles, responsibilities, etc. We never discussed these things and that took a major toll on our marriage. My husband was in school and also wanted to pursue his acting career. I had dreams of returning to school and furthering my business as an event coordinator. We couldn't afford child care, so I had to stay home with the children. My husband was always in school or holding a rehearsal; because we were always short on money, the only time I went out was when we went to church. Jewlz was gone and now Javon was disappearing. I was now the wife and mother. My whole life revolved around my family and what they needed. Because I wasn't happy, I made everyone else miserable. My husband and I were always arguing about where he was going and how I hated staying home all the time. He made me his stage manager and I began working on his current projects. Although it wasn't what I wanted to do, it was his dream so I helped. My dreams and desires didn't matter, I wanted to support my husband. We agreed that he I would support him until he finished school and got his first short film completed. After that, I would go back to school and focus on my business.

At first, working with my husband seemed like the ideal situation. Seeing his dreams move forward made me feel a sense of accomplishment. I knew that my love and support gave him the push he needed. Every time we began a new project, he would introduce us as a team and everyone had to respect both of us. Eventually, that went away. He began talking about "his" play and "his" money. I never felt like I contributed at all. Because he didn't respect me, his cast members didn't respect me, especially the women. They would call our house all hours of the day and night and when I came to the rehearsals, they would act as if they didn't see me. Even though it was my husband's company and I was the house manager, I felt like I didn't belong. Here I was, this wife and mother who always wore jeans and no makeup, surrounded by these model-type women. I stayed away from the rehearsals as much as possible. Rumors quickly began spreading about my husband and various women in the cast. When I questioned him, he denied and accused me of being insecure, and he was right.

During this time, I surrounded myself with women in the church. I wanted to know what I could do to make my marriage work and be a good mother. I wanted to be the strong woman that God called me to be, but I didn't know how. In an effort to save our marriage, we joined the couples' ministry and began counseling. Needless to say, it didn't work. My husband still stayed out, and I was still unhappy. Women were calling and emailing me, telling me about their escapades with my husband and of course he always denied. I didn't have any proof, so although I was miserable, I stayed in my marriage. I thought if I prayed hard enough and lived right, everything would be ok. Things never changed and on our one year anniversary, my husband came home and admitted to cheating with multiple women throughout our entire relationship. I was devastated! Who was this man? More importantly, why did this seem to be my reality? Everyone I loved always ended up hurting and disappointing me. Once again, I felt like God had some serious explaining to do. Was I not living a pleasing life? I never cheated on my husband and I did everything I could to make it work. Why was He constantly torturing me? What did He want from me? Eventually the hurt turned into anger and the anger turned into resentment. I no longer cared about my marriage or my relationship with God.

I began partying and staying out all night. I even had an affair. I didn't hide anything that I was doing. I wanted to hurt my husband. I became someone that I didn't recognize. I did any and everything that I thought I was big and bad enough to do. I even stopped going to church. One day, one of the mothers in the church called to check on me. She said that God had laid me on her heart and she wanted to make sure I was doing okay. Feeling like she was calling to be nosey, I tried to rush her off the phone. When she wouldn't leave me alone, I lost control. I started yelling about how I was tired of doing the right thing and I was living for me now. As far as I was concerned, if God wasn't happy, oh well. I wasn't too happy with Him either. She sat quiet for a long time and finally she said "do you not understand who you are?" She continued on to say that I was stronger than I knew and that my life had purpose. She ended the conversation with prayer and told me that God still loved me, He always had. I fell on my face and began to cry out to God. When I finished, I decided to give

God and my marriage another try. The next two years of my marriage were a rollercoaster. In 2012 I left my husband and moved to Maryland. He moved months later, but we could never make our relationship work. We constantly argued and both were unfaithful. We eventually separated and divorced. My marriage ending was not the result that I wanted, but it was a necessary step in bringing me to this point.

14
THE DIAMOND

When I first realized that I was going to be single again, I immediately began thinking about the possibilities of the next mate. My likes, my dislikes, my expectations, everything. I even began dating. I never sat still long enough to think about my real issues and feelings. I never dealt with how I felt about who I was or my walk with God. There was always something in me that yearned for the relationship that I once had with God but I was afraid to trust him with my heart again. I loved Him, I prayed to Him, but I never allowed Him to have all of me. I felt like although I didn't know what was best for me concerning my life and the matters of my heart, I knew what to expect if I was in control.

One night I was on the phone with my best friend and we were confiding in each other about our past and where we were at that point. We talked about how our past had affected our view on sex, love, and relationships. She asked me if I knew my number. Now for those of you that have never heard the term, let me make it plain. Your number is the number of sexual partners you have had. When I realized what my number was, it was like a "wow moment." We joked about it and continued the conversation. When we got off the phone, I was in disbelief. I sat there for a while, reliving everything that I had been through. I wondered what was wrong with me. What was I looking for that caused me to open myself up so many times? The answer hit me like a ton of bricks: *I didn't know who I was or what I was worth.*

I went and stared out the window of my bedroom. I put my hand on the glass. I must have been sweating or something because my hand print left a smudge. I added another, and another, and another, until I had reached my "number." When I was done, I tried to wipe the glass clean. No matter how much I wiped, the smudges were still there and I no longer had a clear vision of what was on the other side. I realized that my life had become just like the glass. Each time I allowed someone to come into my space, another hand print was added to the window of my soul. My window had become so clouded with the experiences of my past that I couldn't see out and no one could see in. Who was I under all of that mess? What did Javon want out of life? More importantly, what did God want from me? Sadly, I didn't know the answers to those questions. I knew I was a mother, I knew I wanted to be successful for me and my children but that was it. I didn't know who I was on the inside. In the words of one of my favorite songs by David E. Talbert:

You've wasted time looking for real love
You thought you knew what was best
You've lost your will, your focus and your mind.
What's next?
You need to rediscover who you are.
Fall in love with yourself and get your life back.

I had to rediscover who Javon was. In order to do that, I had to realize when I lost myself. I had to go back to the beginning. The only time I really knew who I was and where I belonged was when I was living for Christ as a child. I knew that I had been called to do a work for the Lord and I knew that He was calling me to continue that work. What I didn't understand was how it was going to happen. I kept thinking about where I had been in life and the things that I had done. I felt like there was no way that God would ever be able to use me. I knew that I never made peace with the things I went through. Yes I forgave some people, even asked for forgiveness, but I never addressed the effect that those situations had on me. I reached out to my father and we had a real heart to heart. There were so many things that neither of us knew about each other. We mended our relationship and it has never been better.

Once again, I tried to smooth things out with my mother. It always bothered me that I felt like I couldn't connect with her, especially during my time of spiritual weakness. It was difficult to listen to what she had to say when I hadn't really forgiven her for the issues that we faced and were still facing. One day, I prayed about it and decided to call her. I wanted to know why she hadn't protected me, how could she not know what was going on. I wasn't prepared for her answer. According to my mom, she knew what was going on, but she prayed it would go away. She wanted to keep her family together. I couldn't believe it. I felt like my mother had the power to end my pain, but she left it up to God. God had the power to stop it, but he didn't. I didn't know what to think. Why did God allow all of this to happen to me? What did I do wrong? Was I not worthy of love and happiness, even as a child? God reminded me of the story of Job. Job didn't go through what he went through because he did anything wrong. The Bible says he was *"blameless- a man of complete integrity. He feared God and stayed away evil (Job 1:1 NIV)."* God chose Job to go through what he went through. He knew that Job would be able to take anything that Satan threw at

84

him. The only stipulation: Satan was not allowed to touch his life. Job was treasured in God's eyes, his life had value. It occurred to me that my life was like that. God knew my purpose before I was born. Galatians 1:15 says *"but even before I was born, God chose me and called me by his marvelous grace. (NLT)"* I was specifically hand-picked by God to go through this journey. Not only was I a special jewel in God's eye, but I was built to endure.

Did you know that the diamond's physical hardness exceeds that of all other gems? Let's look at how a diamond is created. Most natural diamonds are formed at high temperatures and pressure in the Earth's mantle. They are brought close to the Earth's surface through volcano eruptions. Even synthetic diamonds need high temperatures to be produced. Regardless of how the diamond was created, all must end up at cutting centers where they are examined to determine how to they should be cut to get the greatest value. Let's apply that to our lives. I already told you in a previous chapter that everyone was born with a purpose, no matter the circumstances surrounding your birth. You are precious, a rare diamond. There is no one like you. In order to reach your true beauty, you must endure pressured situations; however, you can take comfort in the fact that you are never alone. In the Bible, there are several stories about people going through difficult tests and trials; and each time, God was there with them. Take Shadrach, Meshach and Abednego for example. They were thrown in the furnace. When the guards came back to check on them, not only were they not consumed or burnt, but they were not alone. God sent a comforter to them, an angel. When Daniel was in the lion's den, an angel of God was there to shut the mouths of the lions. What does that tell us? We will go through trials. We have to. But we don't have to go through it alone. God is with us, even when we turn away from Him. Everything is for a reason, there is a lesson, or an outcome. The key is to stay in the fire until the lesson is learned so that you do not have to repeat that test. It may be painful, but remember, there is necessary pain and unnecessary pain. Necessary pain is good for us, it is designed to get us to our destination. We suffer when we try to fight the process and don't learn from the test.

When a diamond is first discovered, it is not the pretty, shiny product that we see in the store. Even after going through the high temperatures and being cut to the desired shape, it still has to be cleaned and polished. Even though you may have endured a lot, you can't stop in the process. I don't care if you made bad choices that caused unnecessary pain, you can get back on track. God is a loving and merciful God. He cares about where you are. It doesn't matter what you have endured, or if you have never acknowledged Him before. God is concerned about who you were before life happened to you, the person He created you to be. So many times, people feel like God couldn't love them because of what they have been through. Things occur and we feel like our value has diminished so much, that even He couldn't love us. That is not true. Think about it this way, He loved you so much He sent His perfect Son to the cross to cover your imperfections that were still yet to be revealed. He knew that Satan would attack you and life would be full of trials, tribulations, and mistakes; yet He valued you enough to go to the cross. There is nothing that you can say or do that will ever make God stop loving you. A miner doesn't overlook a diamond just because it is dirty and doesn't shine. Why? Because he knows it has value. A diamond is priceless even before it is cut and polished. It doesn't matter what your dirt may be; addiction, lust, prostitution, etc.; there is a rare, precious jewel underneath. God's desire is to restore us back to the original person that He created. He desires to see His will fulfilled. Allow God to do the work in you so that your brightness can be revealed. Is the journey going to be easy? No. You may have to make some changes in the things that you do and the places you go. As you begin to shine brighter, some may walk away from you. I can't tell you how many people have dropped off during the process, but it was worth it. God has surrounded me with other jewels who aren't intimidated by my shine and I'm not intimidated by theirs. We polish each other. He can do the same for you because you are worth it. Think of yourself as an empty canvas and God as the painter. He took the time to carefully design you; from the crown of your head to the soles of your feet. From the tiniest freckle to the widest curve, God took the time to create you as He saw you. Take pride in who you are, love every inch of you. I once heard someone say that your imperfections make you perfect. It wasn't until recently that I understood what that meant. It's the details that make you who you are. Think about diamonds. Although they come in different sizes, colors, cuts, and clarities, they are still perfect, priceless jewels.

Once you realize your worth, your outlook on life will change. No longer will you settle for anything that is less than what you deserve, in any area of your life. You can hold your head high because you know who you are and who you belong. Now that I know my worth, I see things and people for what they really are. I used to keep people around just to have someone there, even if I knew they didn't value me. I stayed in so many meaningless relationships because I was searching for love and value. Now I know that the ultimate act of love took place many years ago. Because I know God loves me that much, I can love me. I can be alone and be okay, because I know my worth and I know what I deserve. I don't get offended when people treat me wrong, I know that Satan will try anything to stop me from shining. I also realize that it may not be that the individual has a problem with me, they may have a problem with what's inside of me. They don't understand their value, so therefore they cannot appreciate your value. When you know what you're worth, there is no need for competition or intimidation. You know that you are priceless and that will never change.

15
WHAT'S NEXT

One thing I've learned from my pastor is never show the problem without giving a solution. I'm sure that reading this book has made you think about the situations in your life, whether they occurred in the past or if you are going through them now. Maybe your situation is or was not as drastic as mine, but you still need to resolve some issues in your life. Where do you start? The first thing I would encourage you to do is a self-check. Have a real heart to heart with the person in the mirror. Where are you in life? Do you value yourself? Do you know what you're worth? We've already determined that you are a priceless, rare jewel but do you believe it? If you don't believe in you, no one else will. Now that doesn't mean that you get a pass to walk around with a sense of entitlement, but you need to know your worth. Whatever you need to do to get the message in your mind, do it. I have affirmations written on my mirror in my bedroom and every morning I stand in the mirror and say them all out loud. The affirmations change as my seasons change. A season can be anything from a few months to a few years.

The next thing I would encourage you to do is to find someone that you can trust to confide in. So many people are prisoners in their minds because they do not share what they are going through. There is nothing wrong with finding a counselor, minister or life coach to help you sort through the things in your mind. Having someone else's help will give you another outlook on the situation. Writing also helps. Keep a journal of all of your thoughts, dreams and visions. Getting it out of your brain and on paper helps to sort things out. The most important thing you need to do is allow God to do the work. Although God has blessed us with professionals, pastors and friends, there are some things that only He can do. There are some ties that only He can sever. It doesn't matter how far you are from grace, He can and will love you past your past. Romans 3:23-24 says *For all have sinned and fall short of the glory of God, and all are justified freely by His grace through the redemption that came by Christ Jesus (NIV).* We all have a past, but the grace of God is sufficient enough to reach us.

I encourage you to see this journey through to the end. If I had allowed the process to stop me, I wouldn't be who I am today and you wouldn't be able to read this book. I am still a work in progress, but I know my worth and I know that God cares enough to finish the work. Even in writing this book, God polished some things away and I'm able to shine just a little brighter. Philippians 1:6 says *being confidant of this that he who began a good work in you will carry it on to completion until the day of Jesus Christ* (NIV). I want you to have this same confidence. There is a shiny, rare jewel on the inside of you and God wants to reveal it to the world. Are you ready to shine?

ABOUT THE AUTHOR

Javon Antoinette Frazier is the founder of The Heavenly Jewels Alliance, a Partnership for Victims and Survivors of Sexual abuse. She also serves as the Director of Events and Marketing of The L.I.V.E Circle, a faith-based community designed to Inspire, Equip and Connect young women to their Whole, Flourishing, and Fulfilled lives. Javon has a passion for reaching women and young adults of all walks of life through her story of redemption and love.

Javon resides in Maryland with her two boys, Malik Archibald and Cambrin Arnez.

For more information please visit:
- The Heavenly Jewels Alliance
  www.heavenlyjewelsalliance.org

- The L.I.V.E Circle
  www.livecirclecommunity.com

Made in the USA
Columbia, SC
19 February 2021

33222938R00059